A

PRACTICAL GUIDE

FOR THE

LIGHT INFANTRY OFFICER.

A

PRACTICAL GUIDE

FOR THE

LIGHT INFANTRY OFFICER:

COMPRISING

VALUABLE EXTRACTS

FROM ALL

THE MOST POPULAR WORKS ON THE SUBJECT;

WITH FURTHER

ORIGINAL INFORMATION:

AND ILLUSTRATED BY

A Set of Plates,

ON AN ENTIRE NEW AND INTELLIGIBLE PLAN;

WHICH SIMPLIFY

EVERY MOVEMENT AND MANŒUVRE OF LIGHT INFANTRY.

By CAPT. T. H. COOPER,

HALF-PAY 56TH REGT. INFANTRY.

LONDON:

PRINTED BY ROBERT WILKS,

CHANCERY-LANE.

1806.

TO

THE RIGHT HONOURABLE

WILLIAM WINDHAM,

SECRETARY OF STATE FOR THE WAR DEPARTMENT,

&c. &c.

———————

SIR,

  THEY who recollect with admiration and gratitude, the prophetic wisdom and masterly eloquence which distinguished your senatorial efforts, after the treaty of Amiens, will probably consider it a presumption in me to solicit your notice to the following humble compilation.

  And though it frequently may have happened, that those who were gifted with splendid talents have disdained to look down

upon subordinate acquirements, yet, while
your more exalted powers are transmitting
you to the latest posterity, as an example for
the most energetic and enlightened statesmen
to imitate, I may venture to affirm, that
no subject is too minute to obtain your
attention, if it promise to promote the wel-
fare of any class of the community.

In the present crisis the reputation of
our army is an object of magnitude: and the
great importance of a well-disciplined Light
Infantry is no longer disputed, though it has,
till lately, been either too little attended to,
or too little valued. The following sheets
contain selections from the best publications
on the subject, with some additional information, on what reflection and practice have
taught me to hope, may prove useful to
others. I have no motive in this work but
to offer my mite to a service which I value,
as one of the best securities for the honour,
happiness, and preservation of a country,
which

which is as much the envy of our enemies
as it is the admiration and pride of,

SIR,

Your obedient and obliged,

Humble Servant,

T. H. COOPER.

North Walsham,
May 6, 1806.

PREFACE.

THE principal design of the following sheets is to exhibit and compress, for the benefit of the British Volunteers, the whole system of Light Infantry manœuvres, as they are practised by single companies. It may be said, perhaps, that enough has already been published. But as the author is acquainted with no writer on the subject, whose instructions are not capable of improvement, and as he has collected and arranged all the opinions which are scattered through preceding publications, he hopes that the British Volunteers, and the Light Infantry in general, will accept the good intention of an attempt to bring about what can never become perfect, until authority has established a general rule, for the manœuvring of Light Infantry. At present there are no fixed words of command for the discipline of these

troops : Every one uses his own language ;
consequently, very few companies can act
together upon an uniform plan. The instructions of General Dundas have been made a
standard for the battalion. It is equally de-
sirable that there should be a proper standard for the Light Infantry, in order to facilitate their operations in brigade. The author
has in these sheets adopted the most simple
plan, proceeding step by step, from the very
telling off of the Company, to the manœuvring and skirmishing ; paying due regard to the regulations published by authority, and to the opinions of the best military
writers, wherever they appeared applicable
to his subject. But as many difficulties may
perplex the military student, and the written
instructions may prove unintelligible to him,
without further assistance, a set of plates has
been prepared with great pains and attention,
which it is hoped will render the whole perfectly easy and clear. It has not been attempted to describe all the formations of the
Light Infantry, because there is such an infinite variety of them, as would render such

a description impossible, in an elementary ·
work like the present: nor, indeed, is it necessary, as all the manœuvres of the battalion are formed entirely upon the principles
here laid down for those of the Light Company, with the exception of forming and
reducing the column.

Here it should be observed, that though
this infinite variety of Light Infantry manœuvres may appear useless or superfluous,
yet they are not so in reality, as they serve to
render men dexterous, alert, and attentive.
It being necessary that the Bugle Horn
should be used, as soon as the Company has
been completely instructed by *the word of
command;* a selection of the sounds in most
general use, has been added at the close of
the work. The Publications referred to, and
from which extracts have been made, are,

Dundas's Rules and Regulations.

*Regulation for the Exercise of Riflemen and Light
Infantry.—Published by Authority.*   ·

A Manual for Volunteer Corps of Infantry.

Williamson's Elements of Military Arrangement.

Duties of an Officer in the Field.—By Baron Gross.

Instructions concerning the Duties of Light Infantry in the Field.—By General Jarry.

James's Military Dictionary; and some others.

INTRODUCTION.

PREVIOUSLY to entering upon the system of Light Infantry Manœuvres, it may be deemed expedient to treat concisely, on the services and utility of these meritorious troops. The first formation of them appears to have been about the year 1656. In the American wars they were particularly useful; and the mode of fighting, which the American nations pursued, evidently shewed the necessity of such a corps. For, until Light Infantry were established, a regular army was never safe on its march, being always harrassed and dispirited by the irregular troops of the enemy. To obviate these difficulties, the British Generals selected the most enterprising officers, and the most active of the privates, with the appellation of *Rangers*: by these means they produced the desired effect; they engaged the enemy in his own way, opposed

Light Troops to Light Troops, repulsed him
with advantage, and secured and facilitated
the operations of the army. The success of
these troops gave rise to the formation of a
Light Company in every regiment.

After the peace of 1763, the Light Companies were all reduced ; but in the year 1770,
they were again selected ; and in 1774, seven
Light Companies were formed into a battalion at Salisbury, by his Majesty's orders,
to practise a set of manœuvres invented by
General Howe. These manœuvres may be
seen by referring to Williamson's Elements of
Military Arrangement, a book which is now
become very scarce.

During the late war, in 1798, a brigade of
Light Infantry, consisting of a detachment
of horse artillery, two troops of light horse,
two companies of the line, and eleven companies of the militia regiments, then serving
in the Eastern district, were formed by the
present General Viscount Howe, and, by his
Majesty's orders, were placed under the command of Colonel William Scott, late of the
80th regiment of foot, who is now a Major
General in the army.

This brigade, after being reviewed by General Howe, was encamped near the sea at Little Holland, in Essex; where the manœuvres were practised, as they are laid down in this publication, and where the Author had the honour of serving in one of its companies.

With regard to the services of Light Infantry, they are of the utmost utility, and may be ranked as next to those of the Riflemen : they conceal from the enemy the most important manœuvres of a battalion. As the fore-runners of an army, Light Infantry are vigilant night and day, and alert in the extremest degree; they are accustomed to the opposites of concealment in ambush, and exposure in open plains ; have double the advantage of a battalion, from the excellent simplicity of their manœuvres. In the open plain, they can act as a compact body ; in coppices and woods, as light troops ; and in the line, as regulars : they can pursue their course with order and regularity over steep hills, and rugged precipices ; and through woods and thickets, relying upon the activity and gallantry of their files ; they seize upon elevated positions and important posts, with a rapidity peculiar to themselves.

Depending upon Light Infantry, an army has its front, flanks, and rear, secured against a surprise from the enemy. The mode of fighting of the Light Infantry is loose and desultory. They can stop the progress of an army ; and defeat the purposes of the cavalry by their quick and irregular manner of firing. When an army advances in the presence of the enemy, the Light Infantry are in front ; retreating, they are in the rear ; foraging, they protect ; landing, they are the first to jump out of the boats ; embarking, they are the last to leave the shore. The most perfect friendship should subsist among Light Infantry. If possible, they should be permitted to choose their own comrades : for in a hilly and inclosed country they are frequently so extended as to lose sight of their Commanding Officer; they, therefore, depend much upon unanimity, prior instructions, and their own judgment. As the system and service of light troops, differ materially from the

regular regiments, it is essential that a Light
Infantry Company should be composed of the
most active men of a battalion; and to illus-
trate this, the following citations are made
from valuable works * : " The light infantry
" presents a closer combat than the riflemen.
" It occasionally meets the enemy with main
" force, though applied in a desultory and ir-
" regular manner. The requisite qualities of
" this class of soldiers, besides good wind and
" long endurance of quick movements on
" irregular grounds, often connected with a light
" body, and a long fork, are a correct and ready
" knowledge of the aspects of ground and po-
" sition, a mind of enterprise, a bold and
" daring courage—ardent in pursuit of glory.
" The military instruction, which qualifies for
" the proper exercise of this part of military
" duty, consists in a judicious management of
" movements, and firings with aim in all variety
" of ground and position, . . . matured by a know-

* A Systematic View of the Formation, Discipline, and
Economy of Armies, by Robert Jackson. Printed in 1804 for
Stockdale, page 176.

c

" ledge and correct estimate of effect in all
" the variety of circumstances which occur."

" The mode of action, among the light class
" of troops, appears to be irregular ; but it
" has its own rule of order. It advances,
" retreats, occupies positions rapidly, main-
" tains them for a given time, and given pur-
" pose. In short, it meets all the irregular
" presentations of the enemy ; in so far, that
" the battalion, which possesses the great
" mechanical power of war, is allowed to ap-
" proach to its just point of attack without
" annoyance, and without the necessity of
" accelerating its movements ; a cause, which
" produces agitation in the frame of the indi-
" vidual, disturbs the steadiness of the hand,
" and necessarily diminishes the certainty of
" the direction of the missile force.

" * Besides the service which the light infantry
" can perform, during the campaign, they
" may also be employed to great advantage in
" a day of battle ; first, because, it is often
" necessary to have infantry posted upon the

* Count Turpin's Art of War.

" extremities of the wings of the cavalry, light
" infantry ought of course to be posted on them,
" as neither belonging to the lines, nor destroy-
" ing the order of battle.

" Secondly, they may also be placed in
" another position.—There is scarcely any
" battle fought, but where the first advantages
" on either side depend on being possessed of
" a defile, hollow, wood, or some other post.
" The care of these posts, to all appearance,
" cannot be entrusted to any troops fitter for
" the purpose than these, who, without more
" bravery than others, are yet more accus-
" tomed to action, as they seldom pass a day
" without meeting the enemy. By custom,
" soldiers grow habituated to action, and fa-
" miliarised to danger : it may be observed,
" that in sieges they are less anxious for their
" safety, at the second than at the first, and
" at the third than at the second ; therefore
" light troops, who are continually skirmish-
" ing with the enemy, grow accustomed to
" every danger, and consequently fire quicker
" than other troops. On the other hand, what
" may not troops be expected to perform, who

" daily expose themselves, unassisted, to every
" service that offers; when they see them-
" selves supported by piquets and grenadiers?
" If, notwithstanding all their resolution, they
" are obliged to retire, their retreat, which, by
" their continual fire, proves generally bloody
" to the enemy, makes no ill impression in the
" army; it being their custom both to retire
" whenever they find a force superior to their
" own, and rally as expeditiously, and return
" to the charge when circumstances require it:
" on the contrary, when the grenadiers or bat-
" talions are seen to fly or give ground, the
" courage of the troops will be depressed by
" such a check being given to the flower of
" the infantry, that of the enemy raised, and
" the whole army discouraged in such a man-
" ner as may probably end in its entire de-
" feat.

" It is very true that light troops are very
" useful in the field, as they are the only troops
" calculated for skirmishing, and covering the
" infantry and cavalry belonging to the fora-
" ging parties and convoys; they also clear the

" march of an army, guard the troops from
" surprises, and exempt the cavalry and in-
" fantry from many fatigues they must neces-
" sarily undergo, if they were employed on the
" services performed by the light horse and
" light infantry * ; in short, it is necessary
" for an army to be provided with them
" at all events, without considering whether
" the enemy hath any or not. If an
" army is furnished with light troops, the
" General can oppose them to the enemy's ;
" if the enemy is destitute of them, his ca-
" valry and infantry will be continually har-
" rassed and fatigued in such a manner, as to
" be very little able to act offensively.

" It is very requisite for an officer of light
" troops, to obtain a thorough individual

* " The only difference between the duty of light infantry
and light horse, during a campaign, is, that these last can
march with more facility and expedition to whatever part they
are ordered ; in other respects they equally contribute to the
security of an army, and, by joining, shelter themselves from
every sort of danger : nothing can stop them, and they are
in a manner certain of succeeding in whatever enterprise they
undertake."

" knowledge of the men under his command,
" that he may employ them according to their
" intelligence and courage.

" One serjeant, corporal, or private, will
" answer better for reconnoitering openly the
" enemy, that is, for approaching him, so as
" to be able to give a tolerable account of
" the post which he occupies, and of his
" force.

" Another will be better employed as a
" scout, or in watching the enemy's motions
" without discovering himself; and another
" will be found useful by his manner of ques-
" tioning the peasants, and of getting from
" them the best information about the dif-
" ferent regiments and uniforms, and the name
" and nature of the places where they lie, how
" far they send their patroles, their way of
" guarding themselves, the abundance or
" scarcity of provisions, forage, &c. &c. among
" them.

" Another will be better calculated for an
" ambuscade, and have the necessary cun-

" ning for taking prisoners without compro-
" mising himself.

" Others are subject to infirmities, amongst
" which those of the sight must be particu-
" larly noticed ; and even among them, some
" who see well in the day-time are almost
" blind at night. Some old soldiers have the
" genius of resources, and having observed
" some situation or passage, may be able to
" give a good advice, which ought to be turned
" to advantage.

" And as some men are naturally awkward,
" and easily alarmed, it is very important to
" know them, in order not to employ them
" where they might communicate their fears.

" All those different characters may be
" easily found out by conversing with them,
" and chiefly by attending to their reports."

If the reader is desirous of obtaining a full
and authentic account of the duties of Light
Infantry in the field, he should study the
following useful books upon the subject, from

which he may obtain all the information he can wish—viz.

*The Regulations of Riflemen and Light Infantry.—
Published by Authority.*

Otway's Turpin's Art of War.

*General Jarry's Instructions concerning the Duties
of Light Infantry in the Field.*

*Military Instructions from the late King of Prussia
to his Generals.*

Ehwald on the Duties of Light Troops.

*And, Baron Gross's Duties of an Officer in the
Field:—with some few others.*

A

PRACTICAL GUIDE

FOR THE

LIGHT INFANTRY OFFICER.

GENERAL OBSERVATIONS *.

W<small>HEN</small> *Light Infantry* companies are in line
with their battalions, they are to form, and
act, in every respect, as a company of the
battalion.

LOOSE FILES.

W<small>HEN</small> acting by themselves, and not in
line, they may loosen their files *six inches*
apart from each other.

OPEN ORDER.

O<small>PEN</small> Order is *two feet* between each file.

* See Rules and Regulations.

B

EXTENDED ORDER

Is *two paces* distance between each file, or any number of paces regulated at the discretion of the Commanding Officer. The files may be extended from the *right*, *left*, or *centre*, according to circumstances: in executing this, each front rank man must carefully take his distance from the man next to him, on that side from which the extension is to be made; the rear rank men conform to the movement of their file leaders.

MOVEMENTS IN QUICK TIME. *

ALL movements of the Light Companies, except when *firing*, *advancing*, or *retreating*, are to be in *quick time*. They are never to

---

* No specific rules have been laid down for the time or step of Light Infantry, and certain it is that none should be slower than the common quick time; in forming, the charging time should be used. Ordinary time does not seem calculated for Light Troops, consequently a quicker time should be practised, as emergencies may occur, when a strict adherence to ordinary time would be prejudicial; and regularity can only be expected from practice. Timing well, and executing with rapidity and vigour, is the most infallible road to victory; therefore, quickness cannot be too much inculcated in common exercise, which may prevent the bad consequences of being hurried on more serious occasions.

run unless particularly directed, and, in that case, they are only to run at that pace in which they can preserve their order; and it is to be a rule that the two men of the same file, never separate on any account whatever. The greatest care must be taken to avoid confusion, and the intermixture of files.

FILE MOVEMENTS.

THOUGH all movements should be made in *front* as much as possible, yet, from the nature of those of Light Infantry, and the ground they are more particularly liable to traverse, file movements may frequently be necessary, all such to be made from one of the flanks, by previously facing to it.

As most of the Light Infantry Manœuvres are performed in files, it is requisite to add how necessary it is to pay particular attention to the file movements: by a strict regard to this method of exercise, many changes which are now performed by the wheelings and marching in sub-divisions, might be done by file movements more rapidly, and with fewer changes; the greatest difficulty attending it, arises from the ranks not being kept well locked up, which can only be done by much training and practice; the length-

ening out the files is a serious evil, and in
fact counteracts the whole design. But by
due observation, men may be taught to move
in files, much better than they now do, particularly if it were made an essential part
of the duty of Light Infantry manœuvres;
the square could march better, and be more
expeditiously formed, and with fewer words
of command *.

* File-marching is supposed to have been first adopted by
the Prussians, and is thus performed according to the Drill
System. A perfect cadence and equality of step is to be
preserved, and without the least opening out, or lengthening
of the file. After facing, and at the word *march,* the whole
step off at the same instant, each replacing, or rather over-
stepping the foot of the man before him, i. e. the right foot of
the second man comes within the left foot of the first, and
thus of every one; more or less overlapping, according to the
closeness or openess of the files, and the length of step.
The front rank will march straight along the given line, each
soldier of that rank, looking along the necks of those before
him, never to the right or left, otherwise a waving of the
march will take place; and, of course, the loss and extension
of line and distance; whenever the body returns to its proper
front. The centre and rear ranks must look to, and regulate
themselves, by their leaders of the front rank, and always dress
in their file. Although file-marching is generally in quick,
yet it must also be practised in ordinary time. The above
position of feet takes place in all marching in front, where
the ranks are close and locked up. With a little attention
and practice, this mode of marching, apparently so difficult,
will be found, by every soldier, to be easier than the common
method of marching by files, when, on every halt, the rear
must run up, to gain the ground it has unnecessarily lost.

FILE LEADERS.

File leaders must be particularly careful to preserve their proper distances from whichever hand they are to dress to ; and the followers of each file must only be attentive to cover, and be regulated by their proper file leaders. In file, the rear rank invariably dresses by, and is regulated by, the front rank.

FORMING TO THE FRONT.

Forming to the front, is done by the files moving briskly up to the right or left of the leading file, as ordered.

RIGHT OR LEFT.

In *forming to the right* or *left,* the leading file will halt and face as directed, as will the succeeding ones, as they come up to their proper distances.

FORWARD TO THE RIGHT, OR LEFT.

Forming forward to the right or left.—The leading file halts and faces as directed; the succeeding files lead round the rear, and

form to the same front as the leading file
has done, and at their proper distances.

MARCHING TO REAR, AND FORMING.

When marching to the rear by files, and
to *form to the front*, the leading file will
halt and front; the succeeding files will go
round the rear of the leading file, and form
on the right or left of it, as directed. *Forming to the right* or *left*, or *forward to right* or
left, is done in the same manner as when
marching to the front *.

INTERVALS AND DISTANCES.

All intervals and distances must be preserved and taken with the greatest accuracy.
In marching to any point the leaders of files
should take two or three objects before them,
which are in a direct line to the point of
formation; and this may be easily done by
selecting trees, shrubs, stones, or turfs of earth

---

* In filing to the rear and forming up, another mode is
frequently practised, viz. for the leading file to halt and front;
and the other files, if retreating from the right, incline to the
right, and come to the right-about, as they arrive in line;
this seems the best method, as the line is sooner formed, and
the men in action see less of the enemy's fire.

parallel to each other ; and as soon as one
object is passed they must notice another,
and so on in succession, till they arrive at
the proper point of *appui* ; this preserves a
straight and direct line of march, and pre-
vents any curve or irregularity ; the slightest
practice of marching without such an object
of direction, will prove the advantage of
attending to this simple injunction.

THE POST OF OFFICERS.

IN CLOSE ORDER.

THE Officer commanding the company
will be on the right, covered by a Serjeant;
the second Officer on the left, also covered
by a Serjeant ; the youngest Officer in the
centre of the rear, three paces distant from
the rear rank.   If there are any supernumerary Officers, they will be equally divided
with the Serjeants in the rear.

OPEN ORDER.

The Officers are advanced three paces in front of the Company: the Commanding Officer on the right, parallel to the second file; the second Officer on the left, opposite to the second file; the youngest Officer in the centre.

EXTENDED ORDER.

In extended order, the post of Officers and Serjeants is always in the rear, equally divided, where they must pay particular attention that the men preserve their order, and that they fire and load coolly and deliberately; they must likewise be attentive to direct them to the supposed object of attack. The Captain is in the centre.

IN OPEN OR CLOSE COLUMN.

If the right of the column is in front, the pivot will be on the left; and if the left of the column is in front, the pivot will then be on the right of the column.

PIVOT FLANK.

THE proper pivot flank is that which, when wheeled up to, forms the line in proper order. The other is called the reverse flank.

MARCHING BY FILES.

IN marching by files, they shift to the leading flank, to regulate the march. The covering Serjeant leads the company: if marching the right in front, the Officers will be on the left; if the left in front, the Officers will be on the right.

BY DIVISIONS.

IN marching by divisions, each Officer leads one. The supernumerary Officer, if there be one, is with the Officer commanding, ready to obey any directions he may receive from him.

IN DRESSING.

THE Officers place themselves at the third file of the division from which they dress.

COVERING SERJEANTS.

In open column they cover the second
file from their Officers; in line or close column they cover their Officers.

ARMS, HOW CARRIED.

The arms in general are to be carried
sloped, with bayonets fixed. Flanking and
advancing parties may carry them trailed
without bayonets, both for ease and for the
purpose of taking cooler and more deliberate
aim. In extended order, the arms are always
trailed; in closing they should be shouldered
and sloped.

WHEN ON SENTRY.*

When on sentry at the out-posts, to support or slope the firelock is not to be permitted; but it should be carried advanced
in the left arm, as Riflemen do.

TAKING POST.

When a company or detachment is ordered to take post on any particular spot, it

* General Jarry.

is to be the business of the Officer commanding to take the best advantage of the ground,
observing that he must never disperse his
company; but if it should be necessary to
make small detachments from it, he must still
preserve a part of his company, or detachment, as a reserve, on which those detachments may fall back; and this is to be a
general rule, in all cases, where the strength
of the party is sufficient to allow of making
detachments from it.

---

*The following are the Principles by which Light
Infantry Companies are manœuvred.*

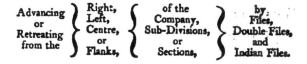

Advancing or Retreating from the { Right, Left, Centre, or Flanks, } { of the Company, Sub-Divisions, or Sections, } { by Files, Double Files, and Indian Files.

FORMING.

To the front—To the rear.
To the right—To the left.
To the front and right.
To the front and left.

Also to *change front on the centre,* and to form *two deep, three deep,* and *four deep;* also to form the *square.*

———

The Manual and Platoon Exercise according to Regulation.

ON THE

DIFFERENT MODES OF FIRING.

WHEN the Company is not in extended
order, all firing is to be by single men, each
firing as quick as he can, consistent with
loading properly ; the firing to begin from
the centre, the flanks, or from the point first
formed. The rear rank man should always
endeavour to permit his file leader to fire first,
and to fire himself immediately after, observing to take good aim.

FIRING, TWO RANKS KNEELING—PRIMING AND LOADING IN THAT POSITION.*

" AT the word *ready* both ranks sink down
smartly on their right knees, and throw back
their right legs. In the front rank, the left
side of the right knees is directly to the rear

* See his Majesty's Regulations, 1st Nov. 1804.

of the right side of the left foot; but the rear rank carries the right knee about four inches to the right. The left legs of both must be perfectly perpendicular. The front and rear ranks respectively bring their firelocks down to the priming position, as hereafter explained, cock, and replace their right hands on the small of the butt: from the left arm being brought across the body, the left shoulders of both ranks are brought forward in a small degree; but the body must be kept as square to the front as possible, without producing constraint."

PRESENT.

" On the word *present*, both ranks bring their firelocks to the present, each man slowly and independently levelling at the particular object which his eye has fixed upon; and as soon as he has covered his object, each man fires of his own accord, without waiting for any word of command; the elbows must on no account be projected."

LOAD.

" Both ranks keep their firelocks at the present, till the word " *load*" is given, which the

"Officer orders as soon as he sees they have fired."

" Then the men come to the priming position, which in this particular mode of firing is as follows:"

" The firelocks of the front rank are in line with the haunches; and those of the rear rank are placed about four inches above the haunches."

" The elbows of both ranks must be as close to the body as possible."

" The front rank men, after priming, bring round their firelocks to the left side, and throw the butts to the rear; so that the barrels may be close to the left thigh, and the muzzles three inches behind the left knees.

" The left hand moves the firelock from the right side to the left, and the right hand is brought across the body to accomplish the loading. After loading, the firelock is raised and advanced to the front by the left hand, and the position for making ready is resumed."

" The rear rank men, after priming, turn the body to the right in a small degree, lean well to the rear, and throw the butts to the front, so that the firelocks may be in contact with the right thighs of the front rank men, and the muzzle in line with the hip bone."

" They then resume their original position for making ready."

" On the signal to cease firing, the ranks resume their standing position, and shoulder."

FIRING ON THE SPOT.

WHEN the order is given to commence *firing on the spot,* the front rank makes ready, presents (each man selecting his particular object) and fires; as soon as the rear rank man sees his file leader put the ball into his piece, he makes ready, and fires through the intervals of the front rank; and when the rear rank men have put their balls into their pieces, each man gives notice to his file leader to fire, by giving the word *ready,* &c. Thus the fire is continued till the signal is given to cease firing.

FIRING IN EXTENDED ORDER.

IN firing in extended order, it is to be a standing rule, that the two men of the same file are never unloaded together; for which purpose, as soon as the front rank man has fired, he is to slip round the left of the rear rank man, who will make a short pace forward, and put himself in the other's place, whom he is to protect while loading.—When the first man returns his ramrod, he will give his comrade the word *ready*, after which, and not before, he may fire, and immediately change places as before.

FIRING ADVANCING.

WHEN firing advancing in extended order, the signal to *march* will be first sounded, and immediately after the signal to *commence firing*; when the rear rank (see Plate I. fig. 1.) moves briskly six paces before the front rank, each man having passed to the right of his file leader, makes ready, takes his aim, and fires; and as soon as he has loaded again, trails his arms.

THE Serjeant of the front rank, as soon as he sees the rear rank has fired, steps in front, and whistles; upon which the front rank (see Plate I. fig. 3.) advances briskly six paces before the rear rank and fires, then loads and trails arms the same as the rear rank. Thus each rank continues advancing and firing alternately. At the signal to cease firing not a shot must be heard.

FIRING RETREATING.

At the sound of *the commence firing,* followed by the signal to *retreat,* the first rank, (see Plate II. fig. 1.) which ever happens to be in front, begins to fire, then goes to the right-about, and marches twelve paces in the rear (see Plate II. fig. 2.) of the second rank, fronts and loads; when the Serjeant on the flank of the second rank sees that the first is formed and loading, he steps two paces to the front and whistles, upon which the second rank fires, and faces to the right-about, and marches twelve paces in the rear (see fig. 3.) of the first, fronts and loads. Thus, alternately, each rank retires, supporting each other. At the signal to halt, they cease firing, and the rear rank instantly closes.

TO FIRE ADVANCING IN EXTENDED ORDER, AND COVERING EACH OTHER.

At the signal to *advance* followed by the *commence firing,* the rear rank (see Plate III. fig. 1.) will advance six paces in front (see fig. 2.) and cover their file leaders, then fire; the front rank men (see fig. 1.) will then advance in a direct line, and place themselves six paces in front, (see fig. 3.) of their rear rank men and parallel to them; and wait till the

rear rank has loaded, when they immediately
fire: thus they proceed alternately, paying
particular regard to the just distances, and
accurately covering each other. All loading
is to be done in the rear.

FIRING UNDER COVER.

In firing from behind trees, large stones,
&c. Light Infantry men are to present, to the
right of the object which covers them; and
in changing places with the other man of the
file, after firing, they will step back, and to
the left, so that the rear rank man may step
forward without being exposed.

DEFILE FIRING

May be so called from being obliged to
engage in a defile, highway, lane or narrow
passage, where no more than ten, twelve, sixteen, or twenty files, can march abreast; so
that, according to the breadth of the place,
the divisions must-be increased or diminished.
When the column is in motion, and arrived
where the firing is to begin, the Commanding
Officer, from the rear, gives the word *halt.*
The Officer commanding the division in front
c 2

instantly gives the words, *ready, present, fire ; recover arms, outwards face, quick march.* At the word *recover arms,* the division immediately in the rear of the one that has fired, recover their arms, and cock ; and when their front is open by the march of the first division down their flanks, they march on with recovered arms, till they have received the words *halt, present, fire,* &c. As soon as the first division has got down the flanks, it must form instantly in the rear, and immediately prime, and load, without halting. Each division must keep its exact distance from the one before it, which would not be the case if they halted to load and shoulder.

It must be observed, that the front of the divisions should not be equal to the breadth of the place they are to engage in ; but there must be a small space of ground, or interval, left on the flanks, for those who have fired to have room to file, and form in the rear. In this manner defile firing, may be performed either advancing, or retreating. The divisions may retire from the front to the rear by another method ; as, after the words *fire, recover arms,* they are wheeled out by sections from right to left, then load, and remain in that position till the last division passes them, when they wheel back and form. Again, supposing the defile to be filled by the division, and no room left on the flanks; then, by throwing back, or retiring a centre section of each division, the retiring division may pass through the centre of the column to the rear*.

FIRING AGAINST CAVALRY.

THE chief object of the fire against Cavalry is to keep them at a distance, and to deter them from the attack. As their movements are rapid, a reserve is always to be kept, and the ranks should be three deep.

FIRING OF TWO RANKS BY INDEPENDENT FILES, WHEN FORMED THREE DEEP.

THE front and centre ranks only fire; the men of the third rank load for, and pass their firelocks to those of the centre rank; and never fire themselves: by this means the front rank men fire standing.

After the caution is given to *fire by independent files*, the three ranks take their proper positions; at the words *commence firing*,

* This looks well, and has a good effect on a day of parade; but it is too complicated to be attempted with safety in the presence of an enemy.

the first and second rank men, present, and fire together. The front rank men keep firing as quick as possible.

* " The centre rank man having fired, shall with his right hand pass his firelock to the man who is in the rear rank of his file; this last-mentioned shall receive it with his left hand, and shall with his right hand pass his own to the man in the centre rank, who will fire with the firelock of the rear rank man, which he will load and fire a second time, when he shall pass it back to the man in the rear rank; and thus the fire will continue in such a manner that the man of the centre rank fires always twice with the same firelock, before he returns it to the man in his rear, excepting the first time.

" After the first fire, the man in the front, and the man in the centre rank of each file shall fire, respectively, without waiting for each other," till the order or signal is given to *cease firing*.

* See page 48, of Rules and Regulations for the Field Exercise and Manœuvres of the French Infantry, by John M'Donald, Esq. F. R. S. &c. printed by Wilson, for the Author, and to be had at Egerton's.

OF

FIRING AT THE TARGET.

In firing at a mark, it is to be observed that the target should be at least five feet in diameter, for, if it were smaller, the unpracticed recruit would be apt to miss it so often as to despair of hitting it; and to become expert, a man should find encouragement, and even amusement, in this practice. Another disadvantage in its being too small would be, that in missing the target altogether, a man could not ascertain whether he had shot too much to the right, or too much to the left; whereas a target of a proper size, with a mark in the middle, being easily hit, the man sees at once the fault he has made, and learns to correct it. The recruit should be taught to fire without a rest, and to begin firing at the distance of fifty yards, and increase it by degrees to any distance.

INSTRUCTIONS FOR FIRING AT A TARGET.

A TARGET should be made about five feet, or five feet and a half high, by twenty-one inches in breadth ; or may be square, round, or in the shape of a man. In the middle should be marked a broad stripe, also two other broad stripes at equal distances from the centre, at the top and bottom ; these stripes or lines should be drawn across horizontally, and of a black colour.

The soldier should be taught to fire at the distance of fifty yards or paces, at first ; afterwards at 100, 150, 200 ; and, lastly, at 300 yards distance.

* " At the distances of 100 and 200 yards, aim must be taken at the lower mark, and at 300 yards, at the upper mark ; the men must fire one by one, at first without, and afterwards, by word of command, when they may have acquired the method of aiming accurately.

" They must be directed, in presenting, to hold the butt firm against the right shoulder, to support the firelock steadily with the left

---

* See page 126, vol. 1st—Rules and Regulations for the Field Exercise and Manœuvres of the French Army, by John M'Donald, Esq.

hand, and to bring the breech, the sight,
and object, to coincide with the visual
ray: and to give them a facility of presenting in the requisite direction, and of
aiming accurately, after coming down quickly
to a present, they shall receive the word,
Recover Arms.

" The men must be told, at the word *fire*,
to pull the trigger forcibly, with the fore
finger, without stirring the head or altering the
direction of the firelock; and to establish the
observation of these rules, essentially necessary, after firing, the presenting position
must be dwelt on, till the word *load* is
given."

THE TARGET. *

" THIS mark is sometimes made in the form
of a man, and of the same size; and sometimes in a circular form, on which are concen-
tric circles, to determine the distance from
the centre; the point aimed at. The distance
of the target, from the firing station, is generally about a hundred yards, and for security

* See James's Military Dictionary, a very valuable work
published by Egerton.

it is placed at the bottom of a hill, or a large mound of earth is raised, or faggots are piled up to such a length or height, as is deemed sufficient to stop all the stray balls. In flat countries, the latter securities are absolutely necessary; but in many places, Nature points out its glens and recesses, where the target may be placed, without any aid from art; and on the sea side no security is wanting. In many places, an old chalk pit answers the same purpose: according to the skill of those who fire in a flat country, the mound behind the target may be made of different dimensions; and instead of a large mound, which it is often inconvenient to raise behind the target, a few small mounds, or piles of faggots, may be raised between the firing station and a small target mound, which will answer the same purpose. Thus, suppose the distance between the target mound and the firing station to be a hundred yards, and the target mound to be twenty feet wide, and twelve feet high, two positions may be taken, one ten yards, and the other thirty yards, from the firing station; and at each two mounds should be raised, between which, if the ball passes low enough, it will be stopped by the target-mound; and if the piece was raised too high, the ball will be stopped by a cross bar of earth

or faggots, over the mounds, at one or other
of the two positions. The width of the aperture, at the second position, or the position
distant thirty yards from the firing station,
may be thus taken by the eye. The target
is supposed to be fixed in the middle of the
target-mound, the person standing directly
opposite, at the firing station, fixes two rods,
or straight lines, meeting in a point at the
height of his eye, and making such an angle
that, looking along each line, he just sees the
extremity of the target-mound. In these
lines, at the distance of thirty yards, two upright poles are fixed, and the space between
these poles, is the opening through which, if
the ball goes, it will be stopped by the target-
mound. A line being drawn between the two
upright poles, and extended on each side, to
the distance of six or eight feet from each, an
upright pole is fixed ; and if a ball were fired
through the space between either of the first
fixed, and the adjacent poles, it would not hit
the mound, but go wide of it. This space is,
therefore, to be filled up with earth or faggots,
to intercept the stray balls ; and over them is
to be thrown a bar, to intercept the balls that
would, otherwise, go over the mound. The
height of this bar from the ground, is found
by pointing a gun to the top of the target-

mound, whilst a cross pole is raised, or lowered, till it meets the eye; and over the bar, at this height, is to be raised a mound of earth, or faggots, three or four feet in height. A ball now directed for the target, might either pass through this aperture, or be caught by the mounds and cross bar, or go wide of the one, and over the other. At the distance of ten yards from the firing station, two poles are erected, in a straight line from the eye to the outward extremity of each mound at the second position; and there, two mounds are raised like the former, and across them a bar is thrown, whose height is found by pointing a gun to the top of the earth, over the cross bar, at the second position; and upon this bar, at the first position, is raised earth or faggots, to the height of three or four feet. It is manifest, that a ball directed to the target will, if not taken with an aim that must be corrected by a stander-by, in a raw recruit, either pass through the aperture, or be stopped by its mounds. If it pass through this aperture, it must pass through the aperture at the second position, or be stopped by its mounds: and if it passes through this latter aperture, it must either be stopped by the ground, or by the target-mound. To prevent any ill accident from the ball bounding from the ground, dung may be raised to the height of a foot in two places, which will effectually prevent mischief. The respective heights of the target and the other mounds, as also their widths, and the widths of the apertures, and of the bars over them, and the distances of the target and the other mounds, may be ascertained accurately by trigonometry. By an easy contrivance, the target is made moveable, either advancing from the target-mound, or passing by it, that the eye may be accustomed to a moving object. This is done by a rope, fixed to each side of the target, and which goes round two pullies, and is drawn by a person behind the target-mound; and when it is made to advance, or retreat, the target is put on wheels, and the ropes going round two pullies on posts, between the second position, and the target-mound, are drawn by the man behind the target-mound, to make it advance; and for the retreat, two other ropes are fixed behind it, by which it is drawn back by the person behind the target-mound. When it is an object to save the lead, a sheet of lead is suspended behind the target, which the balls perforate; and their motion being retarded by the vibrating lead, is deadened by a brick wall instead of earth behind, and the balls fall to the ground."

OBSERVATIONS ON FIRING.

"THERE is no doubt but that the fire of musquetry may be reduced to a theory; but far from that being the case, the soldier has no principle given him; for let the distance, or situation of the objects, be what they may, he fires at random. It is principally owing to the exercise of the target being so little practised, that this ignorance, and deficiency of principle, is so severely felt."

"In our firings, the soldier is instructed always to fire low, yet no reason is given him why it should be so, but that the ball rises. To consider this a moment, the line of level (the line of level is the straight line by which is seen the object on which the ball should be carried to), and the line of fire (the line of fire is a straight line which represents the axis of the musquet), are by no means parallel; for according to the different weights

of metal which the barrel has at its breech-
ing, and at its aperture, so they describe an
angle more or less acute beyond the tube."

" As the eye seeks its aim from the length
of the line of level, it is, therefore, fixed at
the *exterior* of the barrel. But entirely different to this principle, the motional body,
the bullet, is impelled from the *interior* part
of the instrument, and the length of the line
of fire; therefore, the line of fire, and the
line of level, cut each other. From the law
of attraction imposed on all bodies obliquely
thrown, at its delivery from the mouth of the
cylinder, the bullet or ball describes a curve
which, rising from the muzzle, cuts the line of
level at a small distance from the mouth of
the barrel. It will, at about the distance of
sixty toises*, or three hundred and sixty feet,
be found to be at a foot and a half or two
feet, its greatest elevation above the line of
level. From thence drawn to the earth by
that gravitation to which all bodies are sub-
jected, it again inclines to the former line,
and, at the distance of about one hundred
and twenty toises, cuts it a second time."

* Toise *(French)*, a fathom or a measure of six feet, used
by French engineers in fortifications.—A square toise is
thirty-six square feet; and a cubical toise is two hundred
and sixteen cubical feet.

" It is this second point of intersection which is called the musquet shot, or point blank, after which the bullet finishes to describe its parabola to the end of its fall. What is here said is a common property to all fire-arms."

" It follows that, to make the ball arrive at the mark * intended, the sight must not be always precisely levelled at that mark. Suppose a mark, six feet high, divided into three equal parts, if the distance from it is fifty or sixty toises or 360 feet, then, to strike the upper dimension, aim must be taken at the middle one, two feet under the mark; if meant to strike the middle, aim must be taken at the lower dimension, &c."

" If at 100 toises, the aim must be taken one foot below the mark, in order to hit it. If the distance is more than 100 toises, to strike any of the dimensions, aim must be taken above the mark, and so keep raising in proportion to the distance.

" Suppose a battalion of the enemy in front, if at 300 toises distance, aim should be taken three feet over the battalion; if at 200 toises, about a foot and a half; if at 150, aim should

* From this it is obvious that three horizontal lines are better for a target than circles, which, it is well known, tend only to confuse the sight.

be taken at their hats; if at 100, at the middle of the body, &c. Although the horizontal shot of a musquet may be computed at 180 toises, yet, where the fire of a line of infantry can have effect, it is seldom more than at 80 toises, or 160 yards."

LIGHT INFANTRY.

___

WHEN ACTING WITH THEIR REGIMENTS*.

LIGHT Infantry Companies, when acting with their regiments, are divided into two divisions (see Plate XVI. fig. 1—1.): that on the right hand will be in the rear of the second company; that on the left, in the rear of the seventh company, and they will at all times observe the distance of thirty paces. The Officer commanding will be with the right division, also the youngest Officer; the second in command will be with the left division.

LINE BREAKS INTO COLUMN.

WHEN the line breaks into column, if the Light Companies receive no particular directions for covering either the front or flanks of the column, they will wheel as the com-

---

* See Dundas.

panies of the battalion do, and conform themselves exactly to the movements of the second and seventh companies, so as at all times to be in their proper places.

LINE FORMS CLOSE COLUMN.

If the line forms a close column, and the Light Companies receive no particular directions, they are to form by companies, and close up in the rear of the column in the same manner as their respective battalions.

LINE DEPLOYS.

When the column deploys into line, the Light Companies will face each as its battalion does, file with it in the rear; and when the battalion forms in the line, will take its proper post in divisions behind the second and seventh companies.

COVERING THE FRONT OF A BATTALION.

If the Light Companies are ordered to cover the line in front, (see Plate XVI. fig. 1—1.) at the sound of the advance, the divisions

will face inwards, and file from their inner
flanks round the flanks of the battalion, and
at the sound of the extend, or when at the
distance of fifty paces, the leading flanks (see
Plate XVI. fig. 2—2) will wheel inwards towards each other, so as to meet opposite the
centre of the battalion, (see Plate XVI. fig. 3)
opening their files gradually from the rear,
so as to cover the whole extent of the battalion: the Serjeant coverer of each division
attending to the files, taking their proper
distances; the files are to halt and front
themselves. At the sound of the commence
firing, they begin firing as in advancing or
retreating, or upon the spot, according to
to the directions they receive.

WHEN THE BATTALION RETIRES BY ALTERNATE COMPANIES.

THE Light Company is divided into four
sections; the first section is placed in rear of
the first company; the second in rear of the
third company; the third section in rear of
the fifth company; and the fourth section
in the rear of the seventh company: the
whole facing to the left. When the left companies retreat, the sections file, and form, in
the intervals in extended order, dressing with

the right companies * ; when these begin their retreat †, the Light Company faces and moves to the right, so as to cover them, and fires by files, retiring till they arrive at the intervals between the left companies with whom they dress, and remain till they are faced about to retire, when the Light Company again moves to the left and covers them, retiring in the same manner as before. When the right companies are ordered to form line on the left, the signal is given for the Light Company to form sub-divisions in rear of the second and seventh companies of the battalion.

LINE HALTED OR ADVANCING WHEN LIGHT INFANTRY ARE CALLED IN.

WHEN the Light Companies are called in, the line may either be halted or advancing.

---

* This description, of the operations of the Light Infantry, supposes the battalion to be complete, consisting of eight companies, exclusive of the Grenadiers and Light Infantry.

† The dispositions for a retreat must be entirely regulated by the nature of the ground, and circumstances; and over whatever kind of ground a retreat is made, it should always be performed slowly and with order. Hurry gives birth to confusion, and often spreads a panic amongst the troops, which generally produces a defeat when it ought to be least expected.

In the first case they will retire towards the line, closing to their outer flanks by degrees, so as when they come near their battalions they may be in two divisions, ready to file round the flanks of the battalion to their places. If the line is advancing, they will only close to their outer flanks, so as to be in two divisions by the time the line comes up to them, when they will instantly face outwards, and file to the rear.

LIGHT COMPANIES FORMED IN BATTALIONS.*

<hr>

MOVEMENT THE SAME AS IN THE LINE.

WHEN the Light Companies are assembled in battalion, their movements must be on the same principles as those of the line; the officers and non-commissioned officers posted in the same manner, and, as far as possible, the same words of command should be used; it is in their rapidity alone that they must be distinguished, to facilitate which the files are to be loosened to the distance of six inches; but great care is to be taken that rapidity does not degenerate into confusion.

QUICK TIME.

WHEN two or more companies are together, they are to consider themselves as a batta-

* See Dundas.

lion : the senior officer is to take the command. As Light Infantry seldom act in large bodies, all their movements may be in quick time * ; but when in column, the same attention must be paid to the pivots covering, and the preservation of distances, as is done by the line ; the doing so will always be found the quickest way of forming, by precluding the necessity of much after-dressing.

REGULATING COMPANY †.

In marching in line to the front, a regulating company must be named, by which the others must carefully dress, and whose movements they must follow. The officer, leading

* A battalion practised to manœuvres in quick time, will do it with as little discomposure as those who move slow ; soldiers accustomed to celerity, and to move with a quick step, will retain as good wind, and be as little hurried or confused, as those who constantly practise nothing but the parade step.

† " Marshal Puysegur recommends marching in line by the centre, in preference to the right, because the centre is nearer to the left wing. If the centre is the regulating point, a certain degree of convexity must be maintained, to be afterwards reduced to an alignment. In the British service, the regulating battalion is generally on the right ; all the others march by it, and by their own respective centres. The principal attention is directed to the preserving intervals, and the parallelism of march."

this regulating company, must take points on
which to march perpendicular to the front of
the battalion, and must lead steadily on
them, though in quick time; without these
precautions, and great attention being paid
to them, the march in front must soon become irregular, the files will inevitably inter-
mix, and great confusion must be the consequence.

MAY OCCASIONALLY RUN.

A BATTALION of Light Infantry may occasionally be ordered to run, for the purpose
of anticipating an enemy going to occupy
any particular post; but in doing so, the
utmost care must be taken that confusion
do not ensue; for which purpose the velocity
must never exceed that at which the divisions
can keep together and dressed; the distances
must be preserved as much as possible: run-
ning must generally be in a column; but in
a case of absolute necessity, to make a very
quick movement to the front, with a battalion of four of five companies or more, the
best and easiest way of doing it without confusion, will be in *echellon*, by companies, each
retired six paces from the preceding one.

ALL columns of Light Infantry to be
formed by sub-divisions, that is, half companies.

FORMING FROM OPEN COLUMN*.

THE forming from open column to the front
may frequently be done by the divisions
obliquing to the right or left of the leading
division, and, if necessary, firing as they come
up. Light Infantry firing in divisions is to
be always by single men, as directed in
general attentions.

MOVEMENT BY FILES.

BATTALIONS of Light Infantry may frequently find it necessary to move by files
through woods, and over very rough countries : in all cases, where it is practicable, it
is to be done from the right or left of companies, and distances must be preserved for
forming in the quickest manner possible.
Whenever one company *forms*, the rest are

* Columns may be formed by grand-divisions, sub-
divisions, or sections, from the right, left, flanks, or centre of
wings or battalion, and by files from the right, left, and
centre of grand or sub-divisions.

to do the same, even supposing they do not hear the word or signal for that purpose.

FORMING IN FRONT.

I₣ to *form to the front*, the leading files of each company halt and dress, the rest move up to the right or left of them to their proper places.

FORMING IN RIGHT OR LEFT.

I₣ to *form to the right or left*, the companies first form separately, and move up and dress with what will then be the front company, by which means the officer commanding will have it in his power, to keep such companies in reserve, as he thinks proper; as also in forming, to throw them to the right or left of the front company, as circumstances may require; the companies which are to dress with the front company, are to move up to it obliquely in line.

ADVANCED * AND FLANKING PARTIES.

A battalion of Light Infantry marching through a wood, should have parties in front and on its flanks, in proportion to the strength of the battalion. The parties should march in front with extended file, and, if attacked, must take post and defend themselves till supported or called in.

TO SECURE A WOOD.

When ordered to secure a wood of no very great extent, the battalion should go through it, and take post on the opposite side, within its skirt, so as to have the plain before it: in this, as well as in all other cases, parties should be detached thirty or forty yards on the flanks.

FIRING IN LINE.

When firing in line, advancing, the march must be very slow, the line must be preserved, and the officers must take care to point out

* The advanced detachments, the strict discipline of the troops, and the vigilance of the commanders, are the sources from whence spring the most glorious successes.

the supposed object of attack, and see that
the men direct their fire to it; very particular attention is to be paid that the fire is
directed to the proper object, and that it
ceases on the first word or signal for that
purpose.

CO-OPERATION WITH THE LINE.

WHEN the Light Infantry in battalion is
detached from the line, the officer commanding must take care to understand thoroughly
the nature of the intended movement, so as
to be certain of co-operating with the line
with exactness and precision.

TO TAKE POST.

IN general, the method of taking post with
a battalion of Light Infantry, whether large
or small, must depend upon the intelligence
of the officer who commands it, but he must
observe the same rule as was given for a
company, viz. whatever detachments he may
find necessary to make, always to keep the
most considerable part together as a reserve.

COMMANDING OFFICER.

THE success of any engagement, in a wood or strong country, depends upon the coolness, and presence of mind, of the commanding officer, and the silence and obedience of the men, fully as much as upon their bravery.

ARMS HOW CARRIED.

THE arms of the Light Infantry, when in battalion, while in movement, are generally to be sloped, but always by order, and their bayonets are to be fixed.

LIGHT INFANTRY IN LINE.

IF, at any time, a battalion of Light Infantry is ordered into the line, the files must be closed, and it must, in every respect, act as other battalions of the line.

RESERVES.

IT is a first principle in the war of Light Troops, that a considerable proportion of their force should at all times be kept in reserve. The men who are scattered in front ought to be supported by small parties a little in their rear; and these again should depend upon, and communicate with stronger bodies, further removed from the point of attack. These reserves ought, if possible, to be concealed from the view of the enemy.

IN ADVANCING.

In advancing, the reserves must not be too eager to press forward. They must give time for those in their front to feel their way with caution, that they may avoid coming un-expectedly upon a superior force of the enemy.

IN RETIRING.

In retiring, the skirmishers must keep up a good countenance, and avoid hurry. They must endeavour to gall the enemy from every favourable situation, and make him pay dearly for the ground he acquires. The re-serves, if not pressed upon by the skirmishers, will be able to give them, from time to time, such effectual support, as will soon check the pursuit of the enemy.

E

A TABLE*

OF

MANŒUVRES FOR A BATTALION.

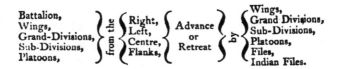

ALL the numerous movements of Light Infantry may be reduced to the following heads :

> Marching in File,
> Marching in Column,
> Marching in Line,
> Changing Front,
> Changing Order or Disposition,
> Forming the Square and Oblong.

* The above table contains no less than one hundred and thirty-four different manœuvres ; viz. forty-two by battalion, thirty-four by wings, twenty-six by grand-divisions, eighteen by sub-divisions, and fourteen by platoons.

All these manœuvres are performed much in the same manner as those described for a company.—See Williamson's Military Arrangement.

THE

GRAND MANŒUVRE.

———

" An army moves on the same principles
with a battalion, and the grand manœuvres
of an army are nothing more than the manœuvres of a battalion on a larger scale."

" Thus, we will suppose an army to consist
of four brigades in one line, each brigade
being composed of four battalions. The line
may then form columns square, oblong, &c.
in the same manner with a battalion; in
which, the right and left wings of the army
will correspond with the right and left wings
of a battalion, each brigade to a grand-
division, and each battalion to a platoon."

" If the army is to advance in columns, it
must be in such a number, as the situation
of the ground, and country, will admit. If
in two columns, it may be from the right or
left of each wing; if in four, from the right
or left of each brigade. The columns are
deployed, and the line formed, either to the
front or obliquely to the right or left."

" As a battalion advances from the centre
of grand or sub-divisions, in order to change
front either to the right or left flank, so an
army may advance in columns for the same
purpose from the centre of each brigade,
or of each battalion. Or to change front
to the right, each battalion may advance
from the left by files, and from the right
when it is intended to change front to the
left."

- " The order or depth of the line may be
changed by doubling up brigades or battalions. It was by a manœuvre of this kind
that the battle of Ramillies was gained over
the French and Bavarian army by the Duke
of Marlborough."

" When an army consists of two lines,
there are intervals in the second line, through
which the first line may retreat on any emer-
gency. When an army drawn up in one line
is obliged to retreat from a superior enemy,
it. may be done by battalions in alternate
line, as a regiment retires by divisions."

" The square * may be formed advancing
or retreating upon the right center brigade,

* " The Prussians deem a hollow square weak, if only one
company in depth. They form them simply : the fourth
and fifth companies close to each other. All the other companies face about. The companies move in square by a con-

or upon the four centre battalions. This manœuvre has frequently been practised by a line of Infantry, when attacked by Cavalry only ; for if they can once get on the flank or rear of the Infantry, they will soon put them to the rout ; whereas while a front is opposed on all sides, the Cavalry can make no impression. Had the French Infantry of the right wing, at the battle of Blenheim, made use of this manœuvre, they might probably have got off with little loss ; a proof of which was given in the following campaign, when ten Bavarian battalions formed themselves into a square, after their horse were beat out of the field, and made good their retreat, before the whole right wing of Cavalry of the allied army."

tinued wheel on a moveable pivot. The sixth and seventh form the left flank ; the second and third the right flank, and the first and eighth the rear face. This square marches with two sides in line, and two in file." See Saldern's Tactics, page 159.

OF

EXERCISING A LIGHT COMPANY

PREPARATORY TO THE

GENERAL PARADE.

———

TELLING OFF THE COMPANY.

The Company, when first formed, should be *two deep* *, and sized from flanks to centre; then numbered 1, 2, 3, 4, 5, &c.; and told off *right* and *left*, beginning with the right hand man, and ending with the left; each man must remember whether he is a *right* or *left* hand file, in order, when the word is given to *form four deep* or *double files*, that he may know where to place himself.

* When Turenne flourished, troops on the Continent were eight deep. They were, in less than half a century, reduced to five deep. They then became four during the war in Flanders. They are now reduced to three, and even two deep. Improvements in artillery, in fire-arms, and the introduction of the bayonet, in lieu of the half-pike, have occasioned these successive alterations.

E 4

BY DIVISIONS.

THE Company must also be divided into *two divisions* or *sub-divisions; three divisions;* and *four divisions,* or *sections* *; and these sections sub-divided again. The centres of each division should be marked, that they may advance upon them if required. To impress the recollection of these distinctions more easily upon the minds of the men, it will be proper frequently to order the Company to form *three deep, two deep, four deep,* and *two deep.*

TWO DIVISIONS.

To distinguish the *two divisions,* the Company should be ordered to face outwards, from the centre.

THREE DIVISIONS.

THE *second* or *centre division* should be commanded to order arms, then the *first* and *third.*

* A section should never be less than five files.

FOUR SECTIONS.

THE *first* and *third sections* should be ordered to shoulder arms, and then the *second* and *fourth;* this will distinguish the four sections.

CENTRE FILES.

THE *two, four,* and *six centre files* of the Company; and the two centre files of each sub-division, or half company, should be ordered to step two paces to the front, then to resume their places in the ranks.

All this should be performed upon the private parade by a Serjeant; and it would perfect the men still more, if the officer was afterwards to see it done himself.

PIVOT MEN

SHOULD be Corporals, or some intelligent men who are best acquainted with the manœuvres and sounds of the bugle; if these can be selected, the motions will be performed with greater precision and celerity.

OF FORMING THREE DEEP AND FOUR DEEP.

COMMANDING OFFICER.		
CAUTION.	WORDS OF COMMAND.	EXPLANATION.
The Company will form three deep.	Form three deep.	AFTER the words, *form three deep*, are given, the third section steps back one pace;
	Right face.	The words, *right face*, are then given, and the man on the right of the front rank, on facing, disengages a little to his right;
	Quick march.	On the word, *quick march*, the front rank men of the third section step off, those of the rear rank mark the time till they have passed, then follow; when the leading man has got to the right of the company, the words *halt, front*, are given, on which each man halts, faces to his left, and instantly covers his proper file-leader.
	Halt, front.	
	Form two deep.	At the words, *form two deep*, the rear rank men of the third section instantly step back one pace.
	Left face.	At the words, *left face*, the whole of the third section faces to the left.
	Quick march.	The word, *quick march*, is then given, on which the men of the rear rank of the third section step short, until those of the right get up to them; they then move on in file; as their rear rank is clearing the left of the company.

59

COMMANDING OFFICER.		
CAUTION.	WORDS OF COMMAND.	EXPLANATION.
	Halt, front, dress up.	The words *halt, front, dress up,* will be given by the officer † or serjeant of the third section.
The Company will form four deep *.	Form four deep.	At the words *form four deep,* the rear rank steps back one pace ;
	March.	And at the word *march* the left hand files step back one pace and immediately following another, side pace to the right.
	Form two deep.	At the words, *form two deep,* the left hand files take a side pace to the left and another forward.
	Close to the front. March.	After the words, *close to the front, march ;* the rear rank steps one pace forward and closes to the front.

* From *three deep* to form *six deep,* the words of command are, *rear ranks take open order ; Form six deep,* the *left* files of each rank will then cover the *right* files of the same rank ; to form three deep again is the reverse.

† The duty of the Subaltern Officers in a Light Company when manœuvring is very simple, and similar to that when acting in a battalion. Their principal attention is to be paid to the marchings, dressings, and to the observation of just distances, and accurate formations ; they must see that the men fire aud level ‡ well, and direct them to the supposed object of attack, and pay due regard to the extension of files : when skirmishing, this forms a most material part of an officer's duty ; it should often be put in practice, to detach a party to cover a wood, or given spot, which should be done instantly, and without any other knowledge than the judgment of sight directs.

‡ The word level does not here imply a direct horizontal line, but is meant to be the line of direction to the object which is aimed at.

MANŒUVRING THE COMPANY

BY

Word of Command.

COMMANDING OFFICER.		EXPLANATION.
CAUTION.	WORDS OF COMMAND.	
The Company will extend to the left.	To the left extend — * paces. See Plate IV. fig. 2. Quick march. Fig. 3.	AFTER the words, *to the left, extend — paces;* are given, the whole face to the left, except the right-hand file, which stands fast : At the word, *quick march,* those faced to the left step off in quick time, and take the ordered number of paces, casting their eyes over the right shoulder, so that each file, when at the proper distance, may *halt, front,* and † *dress,* by the right, without any other word of command. The rear rank men take ground to the right, in order, if necessary, to march or fire, without impediment, through the intervals of the front rank.
	To the right close. Fig. 4.	At the words, *to the right close,* the whole of the company (except the right-hand file which stands fast) faces to the right.

* The number of paces ordered to be taken are generally from two to ten ; on particular occasions the extension may be greater.

† In dressing, each individual will cast his eyes to the point which he is to dress to, with the smallest turn possible of the head, but preserving the shoulders and body square to the front—The faces of the men, and not their breasts or feet, are the line of dressing. Each man is to be able just to distinguish the lower part of the second man beyond him.

COMMANDING OFFICER.		EXPLANATION.
CAUTION.	**WORDS OF COMMAND.**	
	Quick march. Fig. 5.	The whole step off, *close, halt, front,* and *dress* themselves as they come up by the right.
The Company will extend to the right.	To the right extend — paces.	At the words, *to the right extend — paces,* the whole (except the left hand file which stands fast) face to the right.
	Quick march.	At the word *quick march,* they take the ordered number of paces in quick time, taking care to look over the left shoulder, so that each file, when at the proper distance, may *halt, front,* and *dress* by the left. The rear rank men step (if ordered) between the intervals, to the right of their file-leaders.
	To the left close.	The whole (except the left-hand file which remains formed) face to the left.
	Quick march.	They move off in quick time, *halt, front,* and *dress* by the left.
The Company will extend from the centre.	From the centre extend. See Plate V. Fig. 1.	The centre file stands fast, the remaining files face outwards.
	Quick march. Fig. 2.	At the words, *quick march,* they extend themselves as from the right and left.
	To the centre close. Fig. 3.	The *centre* file remains steadfast; the remaining files face inwards.
	Quick march. Fig. 4.	They step off, and as they arrive at the centre file, *halt, front,* and *dress* by the centre.

COMMANDING OFFICER.		EXPLANATION.
CAUTION.	WORDS OF COMMAND.	
		The Company being in the cen‑ tre of the rear of a battalion, and detached from the right wing, it will extend to the left ; if from the left wing, it will extend to the right ; and if from the centre, it extends to both flanks.
		The commanding officer will always signify at what distance the files are to form from each other, before he gives the order for them to extend.
The Company will advance in files from the right.	From the right advance in files.	AFTER the words, *from the right advance in files*, are given, the whole of the company faces to the right, except the right-hand file, which stands fast.
	Quick march.	When the words, *quick march*, are given, the whole step off, following the front file, which leads out.
	Front form. *	At the words, *front form*, the leading file halts, and the rear files break out to the left, and form up successively, in a line dressing by the right.

* When a Company is advancing from the right, left, or centre, either by sub-divisions or sections, it is a good method to halt them, and face them (if from the right) to the left ; (if from the left) to the right ; and (if from the centre) outwards ; and then wheel them into line, which will shew them clearly the exact position they are to take when otherwise forming up; it will also very materially instruct them to pay a due regard to their proper distances, as any deviation from them will be exposed when wheeled into line.

64

COMMANDING OFFICER.		EXPLANATION.
CAUTION.	**WORDS OF COMMAND.**	
The Company will retreat in files from the right.	From the right retreat in files.	WHEN the words, *from the right retreat in files*, are given, the whole (except the rear rank man of the right file, who goes to the right about) faces to the right.
	Quick march.	At the words, *quick march*, they file to the rear, following the right-hand file-leaders.
	Front form.	When ordered to form to the front, the leading file will halt and front; the succeeding files break out to the right, and, as soon as they are on the line, front.
The Company will advance in files from the flanks*.	From the flanks advance in files. See Plate VI. Fig. 1.	THE right sub-division (excepting the right-hand front file, which stands fast) faces to the right: the left sub-division (excepting the left-hand front file, which also stands fast) faces to the left.
	Quick march. Fig. 2.	The whole step off in quick time, following the file-leaders, who remained fronted; care must be taken that the proper interval be kept, which is to be equal to the front of the company.
	Front form. Fig. 3.	When ordered to, *front form*, the right and left hand leading files halt, the other files form up by inclining to the right and left; the right sub-division to the left; and the left subdivision to the right.

* Flank files, are the two first men on the right, and the two last men on the left, telling downwards from the right of the company to the left.

COMMANDING OFFICER.		EXPLANATION.
CAUTION.	WORDS OF COMMAND.	
The Company will retreat in files from the flanks.	From the flanks retreat in files.	THE sub-divisions (excepting the rear rank men of the right and left hand files who go to the right about) face outwards.
	Quick march.	The whole step off in quick time, following their file-leaders, and observing to keep the same distance they set off with.
	Front form.	The leading files halt and front; the remaining files incline * to the right and left, and when in line come to the right about; the whole dress by the right.
The Company will advance from the centre.	From the centre advance.	THE two centre files remain fronted, the others face inwards.
	Quick march.	The whole step off at the same time, the two front rank centre files inclining a little to the right and left, so as to admit their rear rank men in front between them. The Company advancing in a column, four a-breast, the rear ranks will be in the centre, and the front ranks on the right and left on the outside.
	Front form.	The whole incline• to the right and left, as soon as the leading files halt, and close to the front the usual distance: at the same time the rear rank men which were

* In the incline, the rear rank moves in the same manner, and is, of course, regulated by the front rank, which it takes care to conform to.

66

COMMANDING OFFICER.		
CAUTION.	WORDS OF COMMAND.	EXPLANATION.
		in front, fall back in their proper places; the whole dress by the centre.
The Company will retreat from the centre*.	From the centre retreat. Quick march. Front form.	THE two rear centre files go to the right about, and the sub-divisions face inwards. The whole move off in quick time, following their file-leaders, four a breast; the two rear rank front files will incline a little to the right and left, so as to admit their front rank men in a line between them. The leading files halt and front, the rear files break out to the right and left, at the same time: the right sub-division forms to the left, and comes to the right about; the left sub-division forms up to the right, and also comes to the right about: great care must be taken that the files do not mix.
The Company will advance from the right of sections.	From the right of sections advance. See Plate VIII. fig. 1. Quick march. Fig. 2.	THE right-hand front file of each section stands fast, the remaining files face to the right. The whole step off together in quick time, following their file-leaders, and keeping at a proper wheeling distance, dressing by the right.

* Central movements are in imitation of Cavalry evolutions, and were first introduced by General Howe.

COMMANDING OFFICER.		
CAUTION.	WORDS OF COMMAND.	EXPLANATION.
	Front form. Fig. 3.	The leading files of each section halt; the rear files incline to the left, and form up successively in a line, dressing by the right.
The Company will retreat from the right of sections.	From the right of sections retreat.	In retreating from the right of of sections, the rear rank men of the right hand files of each section face to the right about, and the remaining files face to the right.
	Quick march.	The whole step off at the same time, following their file-leaders.
	Front form.	In forming to the front the leading files of each section will halt and front; the rear files incline to the right, form up in line, front, and dress themselves by the right.
		Retreating from the left of sections is done after the same manner, with the exception of filing from the left instead of the right.
The Company will advance from the centre of subdivisions *.	Advance from the centre of sub-divisions. See Plate IX. fig. 1.	The two centre files of each subdivision remain fronted; the others face by sub-divisions inwards.
	Quick march. Fig. 2.	The two centre leading-files of each sub-division step off, and

* All manœuvres done from the centre will be found very useful, and should be resorted to in passing defiles, bridges, and narrow passages. If a battalion has to perform this manœuvre, it should act as one company, and file from the centre; when clear of the obstacle, it may form to the right, left, or front.

COMMANDING OFFICER.		EXPLANATION.
CAUTION.	**WORDS OF COMMAND.**	
		the others follow, marching in two columns, four a-breast.
	Front form. Fig. 3.	The leading files of each sub-division halt; and the others incline to the right and left, and form line upon them.
		The retreat from the centre of sub-divisions or half companies is the reverse.
The Company will advance in line, and on the march change its front to the right in open column of sections.	Quick march.	At the words *quick march* the Company advances in line.
	By sections to the right front form.	After the words *by sections to the right front form*, the right hand files of each section will halt and face to the right, the remaining files will form up upon them.
	Quick march.	The whole step off in open column of sections, the right in front.
	Halt.	The whole halts.
	Left face.	The whole face to the left.
	Front form.	The left hand front files of each section stand fast; the rear files incline to the right and form up in line; the whole dress by the left.
		Changing the front to the left, when advancing in open column of sections, is the reverse.

COMMANDING OFFICER.		
CAUTION.	WORDS OF COMMAND.	EXPLANATION.
The Company will advance in line, and on the march change its front to the left, in open column of sub-divisions, the left in front.	Quick march.	THE Company advances in line.
	By sub-divisions to the front left form.	The left hand file of each sub-division halts and faces to the left; the remaining files will form up upon them by inclining to the right.
	Quick march.	The whole step off in open column of sub-divisions, the left in front.
	Halt.	The whole halts.
	Right face.	The sub-divisions face to the right.
	Front, form Company.	The right-hand front files of each sub-division stand fast; the remaining files incline to the left and form line upon them, dressing by the right.
The Company will advance from the flanks by Indian files *.	From the flanks advance by Indian files.	THE right and left hand files of the company stand fast, the others face outwards.
	Quick march.	At the word *quick march* the whole step off; each rear rank man observing to step behind his leader, the front rank man, so as to march front and rear alternately in a single rank, or rank entire.
	Form.	At the word *form* the rear rank resume their places by stepping to the right of their file leaders.

* The advancing and retreating by Indian files is for the purpose of passing hrough woods and thickets, as well as for the less exposure of the men to the aemy's fire.

COMMANDING OFFICER.		
CAUTION.	WORDS OF COMMAND.	EXPLANATION.
	Front form.	The two leading files halt, and the rear files form up upon them, those on the right flank by inclining to the left, and those on the left flank by inclining to the right ; the whole dress by the right.
The Company will retreat from the flanks by Indian files.	From the flanks retreat by Indian files.	THE rear rank men of the right and left hand files of the Company face to the rear; the others face by sub-divisions outwards.
	Quick march.	The whole step off at the same time, following the leading files; each front rank man steps behind his rear rank man, by which means they form as before a single rank.
	Front form.	The leading files halt, and front ; the rear files form up on the right and left of them.
The Company will file from its centre to the front.	From the centre to the front, file.	The two centre files remain fronted, and the sub-divisions face to them.
	Quick march.	The two centre files lead out, and the other forms in Indian files by the rear rank stepping behind their front rank men as they advance.
	Front form.	The centre files halt, and the rear files form upon them by inclining to the right and left *.

* These manœuvres are principally intended for passing through woods or very narrow defiles. They are called Indian files, from the American Indians, who always march in this order through those vast tracts of wood which they must

COMMANDING OFFICER.		
CAUTION.	WORDS OF COMMAND.	EXPLANATION.
The Company will advance in line, and on the march form different file movements.	Quick march.	The whole step off in line, dressing by the centre.
	From the right to the front file.	The whole turn to the right, and file to the left.
	Form double files.	The rear rank takes a side step to the right, and each left-file man steps up to the right of his file leader, the man before him, and dresses in a line with him; the march is then four a-breast, with proper intervals left for the files to resume their former position.
	Form two deep.	The left files step to the left of the right files, marking time one pace, and slipping behind them. The rear rank closes by a side step to the front.
	Front form.	The leading file halts, and the others form up by inclining to the left, and dressing to the right.
The Company will change its front to the rear by filing on its centre *.	By sub-divisions inwards face.	The sub-divisions face inwards.
	Two side steps to the right march.	The whole take two side steps to the right; then a serjeant will

cross, in penetrating into an enemy's country. It is on this supposition of marching through a wood, that it is the custom for the men to trail their arms, when marching in file.

* " No evolution in tactics is of more importance, excepting marching in line, than changes of front, executed with accuracy. Battles of the most decisive consequences have been lost, or gained, from either omission, or skilful execution of this manœuvre. Had the Austrians, at the battle of Luthen, in the seven years war, changed position, skilfully, on their centre, on perceiving the King of Prussia's attack directed against their left, the well-conceived designs of that sagacious monarch would not have been attended with the brilliant success which crowned the day. The evolutions of that day, drew the attention of Europe to Prussian tactics."

COMMANDING OFFICER.		EXPLANATION.
CAUTION.	**WORDS OF COMMAND.**	
		place himself in the centre facing to the rear.
	Quick march.	The whole move off, and the first file of each sub-division wheels immediately on passing the centre serjeant, and the rest continue to wheel in succession as they advance, each file * forming in the rear of the preceding, and dressing by the centre.
The Company will advance on the † four centre files, and on the march change its front to the left.	Advance on the four centre files. Quick march. See Plate VII. fig. 1.	The four centre files remain fronted, the others face inwards. The four centre files lead out, and the others march to the centre; as soon as they come on the ground on which the centre files stood, each file on the right of the centre turns to the right; and each file on the left of the centre, to the left, and march out to the front four a-breast, covering the four centre files.
	To the left front form.	The left sub-division halts and faces to the left, the right sub-division inclines to the right and forms up in a line, dressing by the left.
he Company will advance in line, and change its front to the right.	Quick march. To the right front form.	The whole advance in line. The right-hand file halts and faces to the right, the rear files break out to the left, and form up successively.

" In counter marching, the Prussians go over the least degree of ground ; and English over less than the French ; whose mode ensures great accuracy, from ing forward in line, to the original position of the front rank."

if to advance upon the six centre files, the Company must be formed three deep.

73

COMMANDING OFFICER.		EXPLANATION.
CAUTION.	**WORDS OF COMMAND.**	
The Company will change its front to the rear, in line, by the counter-march of single files *.	By single files to the right counter-march.	EACH file counter-marches on its own ground; the rear rank keeping close locked to, and filing round with, its front rank man, till the position is gained when the whole dress by the left.
The Company will change its position by counter-march of single ranks.	To the left face. By single ranks to the right and left countermarch.	THE whole face to the left. The front rank wheels short, round to the right, the rear rank wheels to the left; each rank at the same instant, but separately; and, as the leading files meet, they will close to the usual distance.
	Halt, front, dress.	The whole halt, face to left, and dress by the right.
The Company will form the hollow square on the second section; the second section will stand fast; the first and third sections will wheel back on the right and left, and the fourth section will file to the rear.	On the right and left backwards wheel.	THE second section stands fast, the first section wheels back a quarter of a circle on its left, the third section a quarter of a circle to its right; and the fourth section faces to the left, ready to file to the rear.
	Quick march.	The whole wheel and step off together, and are halted by their respective officers.
	To the rear face †.	The whole face to the rear, by the first section facing to the right; the second section going to the right about; the third section facing to the left, and the fourth section keeping its position.

* The looser the files are for this manœuvre, the better the countermarch can be performed.

† The different sides of a square are termed *faces*; as the *front face*, the *right face*, the *left face*, the *rear face*.

COMMANDING OFFICER.		EXPLANATION.
CAUTION.	WORDS OF COMMAND.	
	Quick march.	The whole step off at the same instant.
	To the left turn.	The whole turn to the left : these words should be given just as the right foot is going to the ground, then the men will turn to the left in two paces, and step off with the left foot the third pace, when the word *forward* is given.
	Forward.	
	To the right about turn.	The whole go to the right about and mark time.
	Forward.	At the word *forward* the whole step off together.
	Right turn.	The whole turn to the right and mark time, till the word *forward* is given.
	Forward.	
	Halt.	The Company halts.
	Outwards face.	The whole face as when first formed.
Form line.	Quick march.	THE second section stands fast, the first section wheels on its left, the third section on its right ; and the fourth section files to the front by facing to the right.

As the firings may be introduced after any of the formations, they are not mentioned ; it being entirely at the discretion of the commanding officer.

SKIRMISHING.

The Company being sufficiently instructed in the firings and manœuvring, will proceed to *skirmish*, when one general principle must be observed, namely, that seldom more than one half must be sent forward to skirmish, the other half is to remain formed in the rear, and ready to give support. If a battalion is in reserve, then a whole Company may be sent forward to skirmish as in the advanced guard.

The constituent parts of skirmishing are extension of files, and forming chains; which are usually performed by detachments, for the protection of foraging parties; the escorting of convoys; masking the manœuvre of regiments; covering the retreat of battalions, or forming the advanced guard of an army: and whenever there is a body separated from the grand army, a strong skirmishing party is useful, in keeping up the communication, and covering the advanced parts belonging to that separate body.

SKIRMISHING WITH THE RIGHT PLATOONS IN FRONT*.

The caution being given for the right platoons to skirmish in the front of the Company, the bugle will sound the skirmish; when finished, the † first and second sections move briskly forward fifty paces, when the ‡ second section is halted; the § first section advancing sixty paces further to the front, when they extend themselves to the left so as to cover the whole Company; the ‖ third and fourth sections remain as a reserve. When the signal to march is given, the whole move forward in ordinary time, taking great care to preserve their proper intervals; at the signal to commence firing, the skirmishers in front, conduct themselves in the same manner, as firing in advancing. If the signal to halt is given, the whole corps halts, and the skirmishers cease firing, but keep their ground; on the signal for retreat, the whole corps, except the skirmishers, face to the right-about, and retires in ordinary time,

* See Regulations for the Exercise of Riflemen, from which may be obtained a fuller account of skirmishing.

† See Plate X. fig. 1 and 2.

‡ Fig. 2.   § Fig. 3.   ‖ Fig. 1.

paying the greatest attention to the preservation of distances. The first section, which has been pushed on in front in extended order, conducts itself in the same manner, as in firing, in retreating. On the signal to halt, the whole halts, fronts, and the skirmishers cease firing. At the signal to close, the first section, which has extended itself in front to skirmish, falls back on the second section, which remained formed in its rear. At the second signal to close, the advanced sections retreat in quick time, and take their places in the line.

SKIRMISHING WITH THE LEFT PLATOONS IN FRONT.

WHEN left * platoons advance to skirmish, they proceed exactly the same, observing that the † fourth section is pushed on in front, and extends to the right, so as to cover the whole Company.

The officers of the detached platoons must direct their principal attention to combine, in such a manner, the movements of their half platoons and skirmishers, with those of the battalion or corps, as always to keep

* See Plate XI. fig. 1.   † Fig. 3.

parallel with them, and to preserve the proper distances of the extended order they have been directed to take. The captain is with the reserve, the second lieutenant with the skirmishers, and the youngest officer with the second or third section, whichever advances.

If the whole is to incline to the right, the bugle will sound *the incline to the right;* the skirmishers will then wheel to the right, and the other platoons will file in the rear of them, observing the same positions and distances.—Inclining to the left, is the reverse.

RETREATING ACROSS A PLAIN.

* In retreating across a plain, the † Company will be ordered to face to the right about, leaving the right and left hand files ‡

---

* This manœuvre is most proper for a battalion.

† See Plate XII. fig. 1.

‡ A retreat is much better performed by alternate companies, in a battalion, or by alternate sections, in a company, than by right and left hand files acting as skirmishers, because every movement, where telling off is required, must be inconvenient; it takes up much time, occasions delay, and often produces confusion: whereas this manner of retreating, by alternate companies, or sections, requires no calculation; and the firing is executed with greater exactness.

of each section fronted ; at the sound of the
retreat, the company will retreat, and the
right and left hand files * will immediately
extend themselves so as to cover them, and
follow the Company at thirteen paces distance † ; the intervals left by the skirmishers
must be carefully preserved. The skirmishers
will fire and load, retreating, and without
halting. At the signal to halt, the Company
fronts ; and at the sound of the retreat, the
skirmishers fall in their places in the line.

RETREATING, LEAVING THE ‡ CENTRE DIVISION
IN FRONT.

THE first and third divisions will go to the
right-about, at the sound of *the retreat ;* the
second § division will extend from the centre

---

* See Plate XII. fig. 2.

† The distances of skirmishers, as here laid down by authority, are seldom adhered to, being found very inconvenient,
as their proximity to the reserve will not allow time sufficient for each party to execute their movements with neat-
ness and precision ; besides, in action, the distance of thirteen
paces can never be supposed to afford security to the main
body, however it may answer the purpose at a review. In
general the distances should be regulated according to the
ground and circumstances.

‡ See Plate XII. fig. 3. § Fig. 4.

and follow, firing retreating, at thirteen paces distance.

TO FORM THE CHAIN.

The caution being given that the Company will form the chain *, and the fourth section remain as a reserve. The bugle will sound *form the chain,* when the first, second, and third † sections will advance in line *fifty* paces, and extend themselves to the left in double files at *ten* paces distance from each other.

At the signal of the bugle to march, the chain moves forward, taking care to preserve their distances. The section of reserve follows at the distance of *fifty* paces, in order to give support to any part of the chain that may be attacked.

On the signal to halt, the whole halts and dresses. If the chain is to fire, the signal is made to commence firing; on which the right fugleman of each division of the chain takes three paces to the front and fires, falls back again into his place and loads; the other three men perform the same singly, and by this means the fire is kept up, with-

* See Plate XIII. fig. 1.　　　† Fig. 2.

but intermission, till the signal is made to cease firing.

At the signal to retreat, the whole chain faces to the right-about, and retreats in ordinary time. On the signal to halt, the whole chain halts and fronts. If it is to incline to the left, it faces to the left; if to incline to the right, it faces and takes ground to the right; or the ground on either flank may be obtained by an oblique movement. On the signal to close, the whole chain closes to the point from whence the sound is given.

TO CONCEAL THE FORMATION OF A BATTALION.

In masking the manœuvre of a * battalion, the † Company will advance in two divisions from its inner flanks to the front of the column to any distance that may be directed : at the sound *to extend*, they wheel ‡ inwards, to cover the same extent of ground as the battalion requires to form line upon. When they are to close, the signal will be given to close, and the divisions will face outwards, and file to the right and left flanks § of the battalion.

* See Plate XIV.   † Fig. 1. 1.
‡ Fig. 2.   § Fig. 3. 3.

Or the Company may advance in sub-
divisions, and form the chain; the right
sub-division to the left, and the left sub-
division to the right: at the sound of
the close, the divisions close to the points
they extended from; and at the sound of the
retreat, they form upon the flanks of the
battalion, which will then be in line.

TO FORM THE ADVANCED GUARD *.

No body of troops ought at any time to
march without an advanced guard; and a
communication should be constantly kept up
between the advanced guard and the main
body. An advanced guard, or a patrole,
must detach one or two small parties a little
way in its front. From these, flankers are
to be sent out, who must examine the country closely on each side. The flankers should
keep up a communication with each other,
and also with the party from which they are
sent; by the operations of which their movements must be regulated. The extent of the
precautions to be used, must depend upon

* If the reader is desirous of learning the whole duty of
an advanced guard, he should refer to the King of Prussia's
Instructions to the Officers of his Army, article 1st, page 1st;
and, although it is there laid down for the Cavalry, it will be
found equally applicable to the Light Infantry.

the intricacy of the country, and the probability there is, of the enemy being in the
neighbourhood.

At the signal to form the advanced
guard *, the commanding officer with the
first section † marches in front of the corps,
to which he forms the advanced guard, in the
day-time five hundred paces, but in the night,
or in hazy weather, three hundred only. The
second section ‡ is detached two hundred
paces in front of the first, and a party § of a
serjeant and six men is pushed on one hundred paces further, which forms the head of
the advanced guard. The third and fourth
sections‖ are placed three hundred paces to
the right and left of the first, and even with it,
taking care to preserve, as much as possible,
the above distances from it, and detaching
one hundred paces forward in an oblique
direction to the outer flanks, a non-commissioned officer and six men ¶, who will
again detach skirmishers forward in an oblique direction on their flanks. On the signal to march, the whole advanced guard
moves forward; on the signal to halt, the

* See Plate XV.   † Fig. 1.
‡ See Plate XV. fig. 2.   § Fig. 3.
‖ Fig. 4. 4.   ¶ Fig. 5. 5.

G 2

whole halts, keeping the same position; at the signal to close, the serjeants' detachments join their respective sections; at the second close, the second, third, and fourth sections close and form to the first.

When a Company is in line by itself, and practises forming the advanced guard; it should first be ordered to form close column of sub-divisions, by the right sub-division standing fast; the second sub-division facing to the right, and marching to the rear of the first sub-division. The bugle then sounds, *form the advanced guard,* the rear sub-division faces outwards, by the third section facing to the right, and the fourth section to the left: the first section will stand fast; the second, third, and fourth sections, all step off at the same time; the second section, two hundred paces to the front; the third and fourth sections, three hundred paces to the right and left of the first section, and on a line even with it: as soon as they arrive at their destination and are halted, the officers and non-commissioned officers will then detach forward, and from their flanks, the skirmishers, as has already been described.

SKIRMISHING BEHIND HEDGES.

Suppose a road bordered by two hedges. or other fences, which the columns of the enemy were expected to pass; to prevent, or at least to impede, their progress, the Light Infantry may resort to the following manœuvre. Line the outside of each fence with Light Infantry; as the enemy advance commence firing from the right files, and let each file, as soon as they have fired, retreat behind the left or rear file, and instantly reload. By this method a very small body may keep up a constant and harassing fire, and present the most delusive appearance of strength to an enemy.

REINFORCING SKIRMISHERS.

When a detachment is sent to reinforce a party of skirmishers, without any immediate necessity for its forming in a particular place; the best method is for the detachment to extend itself, and form up directly between the intervals of the skirmishing party; and when called in, will fall back, and close to the point from which it extended: if from the left, it

will close to the left ; and if the first detachment was sent from the right, it will close to
the right: each party files outwards, and
marches to its original position.

LIGHT INFANTRY AGAINST CAVALRY.

———

Count Turpin says, detachments form the youngest officers; they execute in detail, what a general does with an army; therefore, it follows, that every officer should qualify himself for all great enterprises, and learn dispositions suitable to place and circumstances. In the event of being attacked by cavalry, the greatest presence of mind, with determined resolution, should predominate; and circumspection in the choice of an advantageous situation should also be immediately resorted to; therefore, to avoid this impending danger, recourse must be had to the * *square* or *orb*, the latter of which is thus described by General Jarry in his useful little treatise on the Duty of Light Troops.

* The larger the square is, the greater the danger will be, from the probability of its being charged before it can form; for the attack, in formation, generally proves fatal. A small square is more expeditiously formed, and consequently less liable to be attacked before it is completed.

" If Light Infantry are surprised by cavalry on open ground, it must then be de-
cided at the first *coup-d'œil*, whether the Light
Infantry can reach the hedges or other cover
in time; and, if not, they must instantly run
from the circumference to the centre, to form
a round mass *."

" Infantry, armed with bayonets, and formed
into a close mass, can always resist a charge
of cavalry, especially a charge *en fourrageur*:
for that purpose, the men must support, and
press against each other, from the centre to
the circumference, without breaking the *en-
semble*. In this situation, they have only to
present the bayonet to the horses' nostrils, and
steadily wait for the charge. The cavalry
will soon retire beyond the reach of musquetry. The infantry will take the advan-

---

* A round mass or orb, in tactics, is the disposing of a
number of soldiers in a circular form of defence. The *Orb*
has been thought of consequence enough to employ the attention of the famous Marshal de Puysegur, in his *Art of War*,
who prefers this position, to throw a body of infantry in an
open country, to resist cavalry, or even a superior force of
infantry; because it is regular, and equally strong, and gives
an enemy no reason to expect better success by attacking one
place in preference to another. Cæsar drew up his army in
this form when he fought against Labienus. The whole
army of the Gauls was formed into an *orb*, under the command of Sabinus and Cotta, when fighting against the Ro-
mans. The *orb* was generally formed six deep.

tage of their retreat to proceed to some cover, without stopping to fire or load again."

" The true defence of infantry against cavalry is in the use of the bayonet, and in the force of a thick and immoveable body of men, pressed together *en masse.* Horses can neither support nor push each other on, and the force of one horse may be checked by the united power and weight of seven or eight men."

" As from the nature of its duty, Light Infantry is often exposed to be attacked unawares by cavalry, it ought to be practised to form quickly into a round mass, wherever it is threatened with a charge of this kind. Having repulsed the charge, the commander will cause it to march in close column to the nearest shelter."

The following is suggested by Baron Gross.

* " Should circumstances render it impossible for Light Infantry to avoid being attacked by a body of cavalry, they should be formed into two ranks at close order, and form a crotchet on each wing, in which position they will wait for the enemy, the front rank kneeling down, and presenting bayonets ; should

* Baron Gross on the Duties of Light Troops.

the enemy advance to the charge, the rear
rank only will fire at the instant he is twenty-
five paces distance; the front rank will then
rise, fire in the face of the enemy's cavalry,
and after that present their bayonets to his
horses. It will, however, be much better to
form in three ranks when thus opposed by
cavalry, and to keep the fire of the third rank
in reserve. These remarks are only intended
to remind an Officer commanding Riflemen,
or Light Infantry, of the cautions which are
requisite when acting against cavalry; and
to evince the necessity of keeping his men
within such a distance of each other, that he
may be able to re-assemble them in time, and
the propriety of having a reserve behind him,
to form a third rank, in case it should be
wanted."

THE disposition for a detachment of Infantry, retreating in a plain from before
cavalry, much superior to it, is thus described
by Count Turpin :—

" Suppose five hundred foot retreating from
" before a thousand horse; the foot may re-
" treat in a square, the four angles being co-
" vered on the outside by grenadiers: these gre-
" nadiers should preserve their fire till the horse
" come so near, that they are in danger of be-

" ing broke in upon, unless they can keep them
" at a distance by firing upon them. The
" fire of this square should be carefully mana-
" ged and given by the platoons, when the
" horse is within the distance of thirty paces;
" for if the enemy is permitted to come
" nearer, the soldier, incapable of reasoning
" like an officer, is often more frightened at
" the horse than the man; and being too much
" confused to present his piece, and fire pro-
" perly, will fall back, and consequently
" make an opening in the battalion, through
" which resolute cavalry will not fail to enter;
" whereas, when the enemy is at thirty paces
" distance, he is not yet near enough to inti-
" midate the soldier, but is at a proper di-
" stance for the fire to have the wished effect.
" But even suppose, for a moment, that the
" soldier is not frightened at this great body
" of cavalry coming down upon him, and
" waits for it till it is almost within reach of
" his bayonet, in order to make a surer
" fire, and at the same time to thrust his bay-
" onet into the horse's breast; as it is the na-
" ture of a horse, when killed, to fall forwards,
" or, when wounded, to push upon that part
" from whence the blow came, the soldier is
" of course obliged to give way, to make
" room for the killed or wounded horse;

" therefore if only one horse, dead or alive,
" gets into the ranks, the square is broken;
" which is one of the reasons for not suffering
" the enemy to approach nearer than thirty
" paces; and the fire, if well directed, will
" have its full effect at that distance, and the
" killed or wounded horses will not be within
" reach of breaking the square. The reason
" why the square should not fire by divisions
" is, in case any troops of horse should re-
" main unbroken, and continue the charge,
" they will find a fire from every part, which
" will, in all probability, at last force them to
" retire in disorder, to a distance from the
" square. But notwithstanding, for many
" reasons above mentioned, the disposition
" in column is always preferable to that of
" a square: five hundred foot will form a
" column sufficient to retreat with safety, and
" keep up a constant fire.

" If the detachment is stronger in infantry,
" and the enemy proportionably superior, a co-
" lumn is best, because the column being full,
" forms a body that must act together, and of
" which all the evolutions are uniform; an ad-
" vantage not to be found in a square, as there
" will be a great void in the centre, and one
" side of the square may march faster or slower
" than the other three, which may cause an

" opening at two of the angles, although
" guarded by grenadiers.

" Suppose a detachment of twelve hundred
" foot, retreating in an open country, attacked
" by two thousand horse; the disposition in
" column is imagined to be the best it can
" take. This column shall have sixteen men
" in front, and sixty-two in depth; the re-
" maining two hundred and eight, supposed
" to be grenadiers, shall be divided into four
" parts; two of which will support the two
" flanks at the head, the two others, those of
" the rear guard : by this disposition it is ima-
" gined the infantry will be enabled to make
" a good retreat. If the enemy should attack
" but one side, by firing in the manner above
" directed, he will certainly lose great num-
" bers before he will be able to come near the
" column ; besides, the depth of the column
" occupying far less ground than the enemy's
" cavalry, unless he forms himself in four
" or five lines, the infantry can never be
" engaged but with the first line. Those in
" the rear not adding to the weight of the
" charge, it must be impossible for rear ranks
" of cavalry to add to the force; the success
" of the attack chiefly depending upon the
" quickness with which the troopers in the
" front rank charge; thus the column of in-

" fantry is stronger in itself, than the line of
" cavalry by which it is attacked.

" If the enemy should attack the two flanks,
" then the column, by making a motion to the
" right or left, will be formed in eight ranks
" on one side, and eight on the other; and if
" the advanced or the rear guard is attacked, it
" will then be the grenadiers inclusive, thirty-
" four men in front. Thus it appears that, on
" whatever side the column is attacked, it
" will be in force, and capable of resisting
" so superior an enemy.

" The detachment should be caused to ob-
" serve a profound silence; so that the
" firings, when ordered, may be executed with
" the utmost exactness. It is the officer's
" duty to make the platoons they command
" obey, and to prevent them from firing till
" they judge proper; for it is very certain,
" if the soldiers are left to themselves, they
" will be firing continually; and the column
" having thrown away its fire would prevent
" so favourable a moment for the enemy to
" make the attack, having nothing to fear
" but the bayonet, that he would scarcely
" fail seizing the opportunity: but if care
" hath been taken to preserve the fire, and
" to fire by * platoons only, it is morally cer-

* Platoon and Company are synonimous terms.

" tain that a column in this disposition can
" retreat safely from before a body of ca-
" valry. very superior. If the enemy can be
" prevented breaking into the column at the
" first charge, it is very certain his ardour
" will be greatly abated in the second, and
" still more in the third, till at length he
" shall be repulsed with great loss, and the
" detachments perhaps escape without losing
" a man."

SIGNALS.

In the Rules and Regulations it is particularly mentioned, that words of command are on all occasions to be used, and that signals are only to be resorted to in aid of the voice.

The necessary signals are to be few and simple, and should be well understood by the Officers and non-commissioned Officers.

All signals are to be repeated ; and those made from the line or column are to convey the intentions of the Commanding Officer of the line or column to the Officer commanding the Light Infantry, who will communicate them to the several companies or detachments either by word or signal.

At the commencement of the sound of the bugle (if on the march) the Company should mark time, and never begin to change their position till the sound is quite finished.

When any change is to take place from the right, left, or centre of the Company, the low G is generally made use of as a caution, and is sounded previous to the other notes; if from the right, two G's are to be sounded;

H

if from the left, three G's are to be sounded; and if from the centre, one G *.

A good bugle may be heard at the distance of three miles.

The following are the Signals for the Bugle and Drum, which are to be considered as fixed and determined ones.

FOR THE BUGLE.

To Advance.
To Retreat.
To Halt.
To Cease Firing.
To Assemble.

FOR THE DRUM.

To Advance, ... Grenadiers March.
To Retreat, ... The Retreat.
To Halt, ... Troop.
To Cease Firing, ... The General.
To Assemble, ... To Arms.

* See a very useful little work published by Egerton, entitled, The Bugle Horn Sounds, as used by the 95th, or Rifle Regiment.

EXPLANATION OF THE PLATES.

ALL the Plates, excepting that of the advanced guard, represent twenty files, two deep, and these are divided into two subdivisions of ten files each; and four sections, of five files to each section; a number quite sufficient to answer the intended purpose. No serjeants are exhibited in any of the Plates, excepting that of the advanced guard, in order that the officers may be the better distinguished: they can easily be represented in the mind, by supposing, at close order, the officers to be covered, and in extended order the serjeants to be equally divided in the rear; to have personated them would have tended to very little purpose, and only added to the confusion and expence of the engravings. The whole of the Company is supposed to be reviewed with its officers complete.

The officers are distinguished by their swords drawn.
The front rank men are numbered.
The front and line of march are indicated by the arrows and dotted lines.
Serjeants in the advanced guard are represented by the initial S.

INDEX.

INDEX.

INDEX.

INDEX.

THE END.

R. WILKS, PRINTER, CHANCERY-LANE.

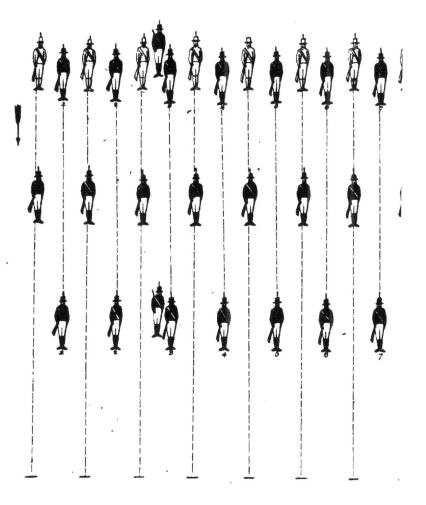

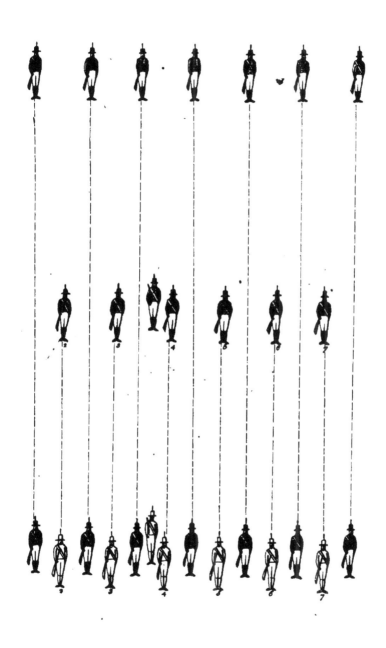

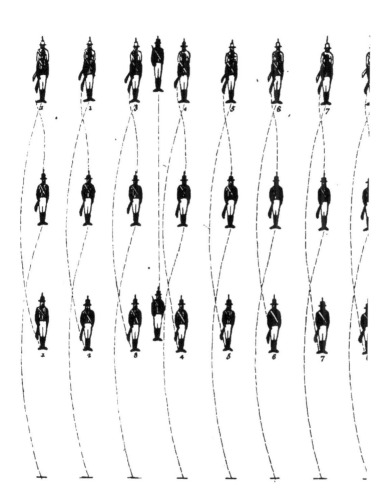

Fig. 2.

Facing to the Left previous to extending from the R.

Fig. 5.

Company Formed.

T.H. Cooper delin.ᵗ·   Hixon sculp.!

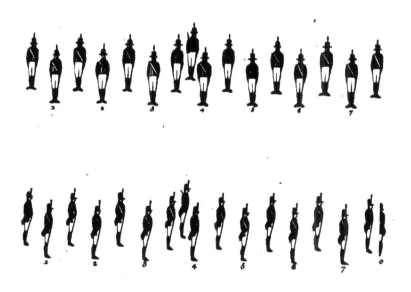

Pl. 6.

Facing Outwa

Fig:1.

Fig: 2.

Marching in Files from th

Fig:3.

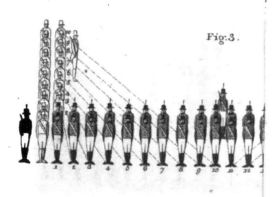

Forming to the Fr

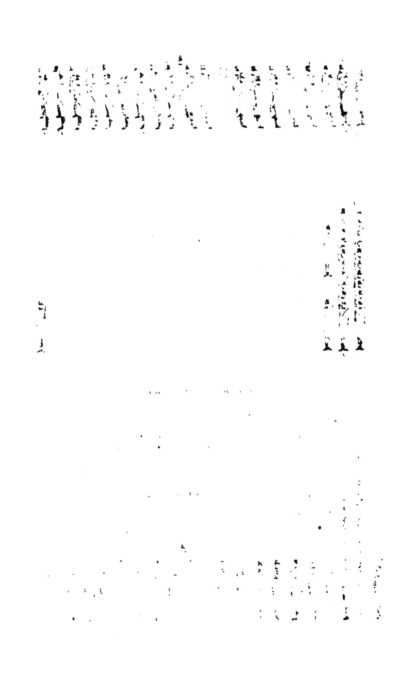

Faced inwards to

F

Column

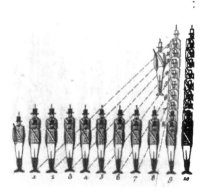

T.H. Cooper del.ᵗ

Forming Line upon the

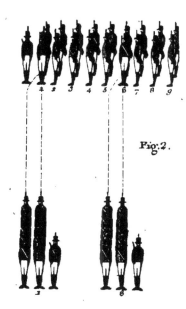

Fig. 2.

Fig. 3.

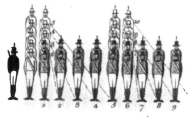

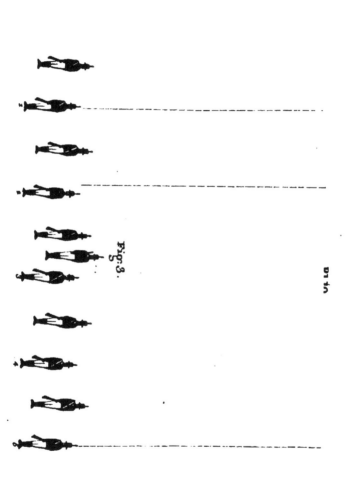

Fig. 3.

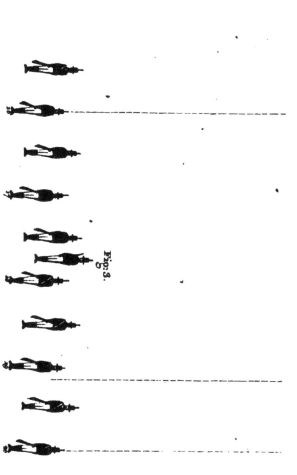

Fig. 3.

Skirmishing with the Left Platoons in front.

T. H. Coper delin.t

Hixon sculp.t

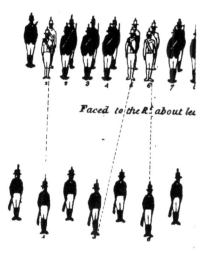

Faced to the R. about le...

Right and left han...

Faced to the R. abo...

Center divisio...

covering ...

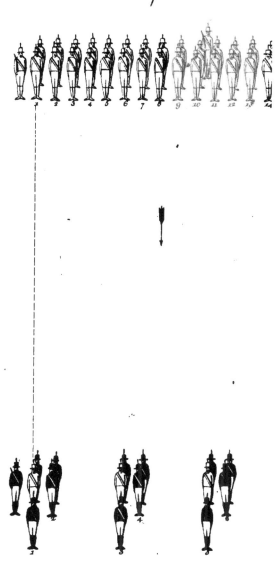

Formation of the Chain?

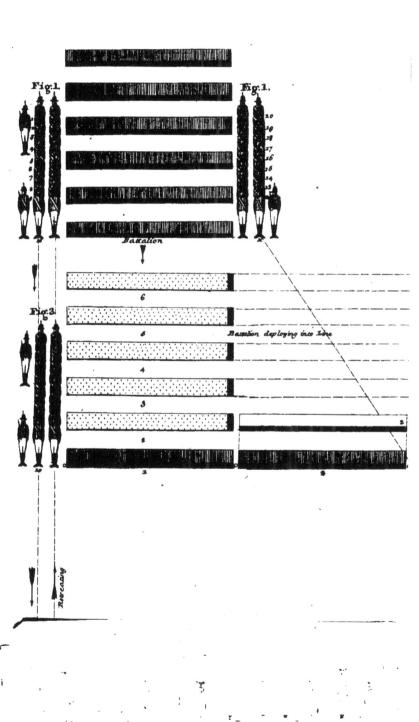

Fig.1.

Fig.1.

Battalion

Battalion deploying into Line

Fig.3.

Retreating

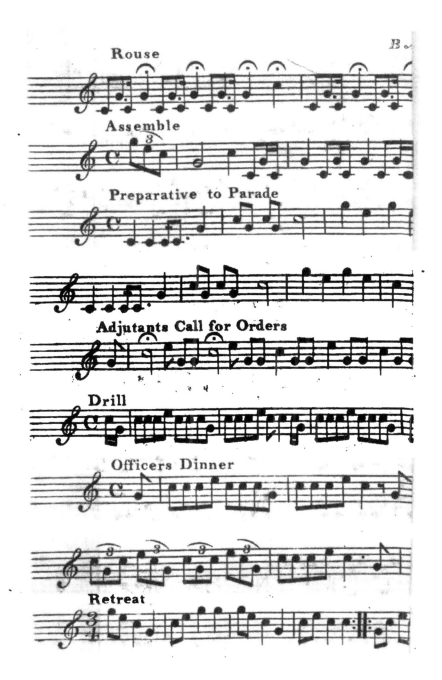

Lightning Source UK Ltd.
Milton Keynes UK
UKHW020623180722
406010UK00006B/824